Family And Educator's Guide

To Accompany

The House Where Happiness Lived

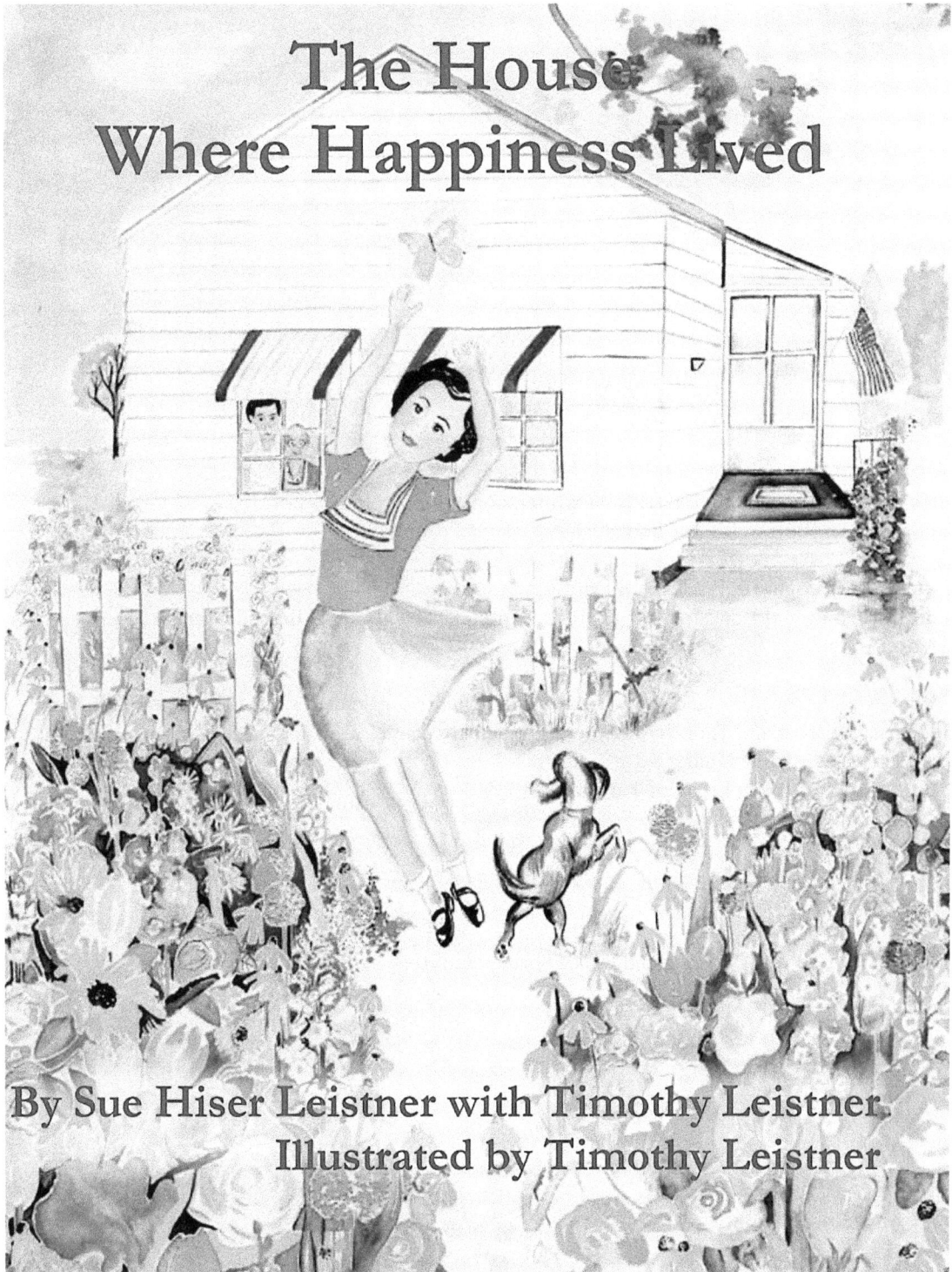

By Sue Hiser Leistner with Timothy Leistner
Illustrated by Timothy Leistner

Guide written and illustrated by Timothy Leistner, Ed.D.
Curricular activities to increase understanding. For All Ages

Library of Congress Cataloging in Publication Data
Leistner, Timothy, Family and Educator's Guide to Accompany The House Where Happiness Lived.
"A Button Bucket Book."

Summary: A family and educator's guide to accompany the children's picture book, "The House Where Happiness Lived" by Sue Hiser Leistner and Timothy Leistner. Fundamental and useful activities to promote understanding.
(1. Happiness-Fiction. 2. Family-Guide)
I. Leistner, Timothy, ill. II. Title, Leistner, Timothy 2013.

ISBN ;9780615950006

Model credits: Thank you to Jeff, Norah, and Grace Shriner and Renee and Isaiah Maniscalco

Button Bucket Books

TABLE OF
C O N T E N T S

Dedication

For Sue Hiser Leistner, "always"

FORWARD:

This Family and Educators' Guide has been created to complement the book, "**The House Where Happiness Lived**" by Sue Hiser Leistner and Timothy Leistner. The guide includes valuable information for parents and teachers, including strategies to inspire a love for reading and ways to use children's picture books at home or in the classroom. This guide is a means to make literature come alive for children.

Stories take us on a excursion and allow us to visit new places and other times where we meet new character friends and learn from the experiences in their lives. Reading and listening to literature read aloud helps us develop an appreciation for reading and learning.

Within this guide you will find loads of fun activity ideas, which will help children to extend learning and reinforce developing concepts. Activities within the guide are appropriate for use at home or at school. Teachers will find the sample lesson plan and each of the hands-on activities useful. Parents will enjoy reading aloud with their child, completing the activities together, and utilizing A Month of Fun Family Activities. The guide includes concepts for learning about and evaluating narrative children's books; useful extension activities; ideas for further study; and more.

While completing the activities within the guide, children will listen, read, write, speak and discuss, visually represent, create, and develop critical thinking abilities. Most importantly they will develop further understanding and the enjoyment that comes from reading. Use the activities to reinforce literacy concepts, further comprehension, acquire new vocabulary, and to simply enjoy completing the activities and have fun!
Enjoy the book, "The House Where Happiness Lived" and share happiness!

ABOUT THE BOOK:

"**The House Where Happiness Lived**" by Sue Hiser Leistner and Timothy Leistner is a heartwarming family story about a young child who finds happiness through helping and sharing with her family and neighbors. It is a timeless story about family, happiness, and love. The children's picture book is geared for pre-kindergarten through third grade children, yet no matter what age, this timeless tale focuses on the value of family and the true foundation of happiness. Nowadays, it's welcoming theme of helping and caring is as vital as ever!

The story's genre is considered Historical Fiction, however it is actually about the lives of real life people. The story is set during the ending years of the Great Depression in the USA and provides children with a narrative and history lesson about the time.

READ ALOUD!

The Importance of Reading Aloud with Children cannot be overemphasized. Reading aloud with children is one of the best ways to help develop an interest in reading, model reading, promote language, advance language arts skills, and support a child's emergent reading development. Reading together helps advance language comprehension skills and word recognition skills. When parents and teachers read aloud with children they are forging a pathway towards a love of reading and developing lifelong readers. Reading aloud together is fun too! Yet, sadly, many parents do not read aloud with their children. Experts say parents and teachers should read aloud with children every day from infancy and throughout the child's preschool and school years. The first eight years of a child's life are critical for literacy development. Babies enjoy the sound of your voice and the rhythmic language that good books provide; toddlers enjoy lap time stories and the closeness of being together while you read a book; school age children love story times and time to discuss books; and older children benefit from sharing stories as well. The length of time we should read aloud to children varies depending on the age of the child. Babies may enjoy a short five-minute story before naptime; while kindergarten children may enjoy 20-30 minutes of story time; and the length of time should increase as the child grows. Young children enjoy listening to an adult reading a story to them. But don't stop reading aloud after children are old enough to read by themselves. Older children, yes, even teenagers, benefit from reading together. Older children who read to younger siblings and friends benefit from reading aloud to others. Realize that even senior citizens love to hear a story read aloud to them. So, start reading and continue reading aloud together throughout life. Read aloud advice:

- Share "read-aloud stories" with children from the beginning and throughout life.
- Read aloud every day - together!
- Demonstrate and model reading to children.
- Read books which are appropriate for your child's age level and interests.
- Talk with your child about the stories in books, making eye contact, and connecting the stories to the child's personal life.
- Reveal the various purposes for reading (reading for knowledge, information, communication, study, research, safety, and pleasure).
- Give children a variety of books providing them with a balance of literary genres.
- Connect books with your daily routines. (Add books to every room of your home).
- Join your local neighborhood library and make frequent visits to get new books.
- Read together as a "Family Experience." Talk, share family stories, and discuss books.

READ ALOUD LESSON PLAN - EXAMPLE:

Literature Source: *The House Where Happiness Lived* (Sue Hiser Leistner & Timothy Leistner).

Summary: The "Child of Happiness" finds happiness by doing good things for others in this delightful story about family, everyday adventures, and love.

Instructional Objectives/ Results

Specific Learning Objectives: The learner will...

- listen to the read aloud presentation to identify details within the story. (Listening, Speaking)
- listen to the story to correctly retell the sequence of events. (Listening, Speaking)
- verbally identify at least one difference between the time period for which the story is set and the present time. (Thinking, Speaking)
- demonstrate understanding of characters and supporting evidence through discussion. (Thinking, Speaking)
- listen to the story to correctly answer comprehension questions. (Listening, Thinking, Speaking)
- interpret and illustrate a picture about the story. (Visual representing)

Standards:

Common Core Standards (K-3)

CCSS. ELA-Literacy. RL.K.1 With prompting and support, ask and answer questions about key details in a text.

RL.1.1 Ask and answer questions about key details in a text.

RL.2.1 Ask and answer such questions as *who, what, where, when, why*, and *how* to demonstrate understanding of key details in a text.

RL.3.1 Ask and answer questions to demonstrate understanding of a text, referring explicitly to the text as the basis for the answers.

CCSS. ELA-Literacy. RL.K.3 With prompting and support, identify characters, setting, and major events in a story.

RL 1.3 Describe characters, settings, and major events in a story, using key details.

Rl.2.3 Describe how characters in story respond to major events and challenges.

RL.3.3 Describe characters in a story (e.g., their traits, motivations, or feelings) and explain how their actions contribute to the sequence of events.

CCSS.ELA-Literacy. RL.K.7 With prompting and support, describe the relations between illustration and story in which they appear (e.g., what moment in a story an illustration depicts).

RL.1.7 Use illustrations and details in a story to describe its characters, setting or events.

RL.2.7 Use information gained from the illustrations and words in a print or digital text to demonstrate understanding of its characters, setting, or plot.

CCSS.ELA-Literacy.RL.3.7 Explain how specific aspects of a text's illustrations contribute to what is conveyed by the words in a story (e.g., create mood, emphasize aspects of a character or setting).

CCSS. ELA-Literacy. RL.K.9 With prompting and support, compare and contrast the adventures and experiences of characters in familiar stories.

RL 1.9 Compare and contrast the adventures and experiences of characters in stories.

VA-Visual arts. The student will analyze, reflect on, and apply the structures of art. VA standard 4.3. a. Contextualizing: The student will interpret and apply visual arts in relation to cultures, history, and all learning. Recognize the connection of visual arts to all learning. Use a visual arts form as help in expressing an idea in a nonart subject; e.g., a social studies project.

_____ National Governors Association Center for Best Practices. *Common core state standards.*

Goal 3 Standards
Standard 1 Information Manger
Standard 2 Effective Communicator
Standard 4 Creative and Critical Thinker

ESOL Standards
Students read a wide range of print and non-print texts to build understanding of texts, themselves, and of the cultures of the United States and the world; to acquire new information; to respond to the needs and demands of society and the workplace; and for personal fulfillment. Among these texts are fiction and nonfiction, classic and contemporary works. (NCTE)
Standard 1: Students will listen, speak, read, and write in English for information and understanding. 1. Identify and use basic reading and listening strategies to make text comprehensible and meaningful. (LR)
2. View, listen to, read, gather, organize and discuss information from various sources.
Standard 2: Students will listen, speak, read, and write in English for literary response, enjoyment, and expression. 2. Use basic reading and listening strategies to make literary text comprehensible and meaningful. 4. Identify key literary elements in texts and relate those features to students' own experiences. (SR)
_____ National Council of Teachers of English. *Standards for English Language Arts*.

Subject Matter Content
Listening to a story read aloud motivates the listener to learn more about the characters, setting, time period, and the plot of the story. The language encourages the reader (listener) to visualize the images.

Instructional Methods
Lesson Introducing Activities
- The teacher holds up and displays the book so that students can see the front cover and asks the students, "Look at the front cover of the book. From the cover illustration (the picture), what do you think the story will be about?" Discuss.
- Teacher asks, "Who is the author?" "What does an author do?"
  "Who is the illustrator?" "What does an illustrator do?"
- Teacher reads the title: "The House Where Happiness Lived" to students. The teacher builds on the students' prior knowledge by asking: What is a house? Who lives in houses? Where do you live? Are there different types of houses? Who lives in them? Discuss.

Fundamental Activities
- The teacher reads the book aloud to the students.
- The teacher and learners discuss the story. The teacher asks learners questions regarding specific details within the story; the sequence of events within the story; characters; and comprehension questions.

Conclusion Activities
- Teachers may use chart paper and a marker to discuss and compare and contrast the time period set in the story and the present time.
- The teacher provides drawing paper and art materials for students to illustrate a picture interpreting an event within the story.
- Students complete their own personal illustrations.

Materials and Equipment:
The House Where Happiness Lived by Sue Hiser Leistner with Timothy Leistner
Drawing (illustration) paper
Crayons, markers, and/or colored pencils
Chart paper and marker
Character Stick Puppets (see template within this guide)

Assessment & Evaluation Using the following assessment tool, evaluate how well students met each of the specific learning objectives:

Read Aloud-Listening Checklist Rubric	1	2	3	Total points
The student listens to the story and participated in the discussion	Does not listen nor attend	Attends, listens, and participates	Actively attends, listens, and participates	
Identifies details within the story	Does not recall nor site details within the story	Verbally sites some detail from the reading	Verbally sites details within the story with understanding	
Correctly retells the sequence of events	Does not retell sequence of events	Retells sequence of events with some errors	Retells sequence of events with few or no errors	
Verbally identifies at least one difference between the time period for which the story is set and the present time	Makes significant errors. Responses are unclear	Verbally identifies at least one difference. Answers are mostly clear	Verbally identifies one or more differences. Answers are clear	
Demonstrate understanding of characters and provides supporting evidence through discussion	Cannot identify any characters nor provide understanding Answers are unclear	Verbally identifies at least one character and some supporting evidence.	Verbally identifies the characters and provides clear supporting evidence	
Correctly answer comprehension questions	Makes significant errors. Responses are unclear	Makes few mistakes answering questions. Answers are mostly clear	Correctly answers questions with clear responses	
Interprets and illustrates a picture about the story (Product: Picture about the story)	Does not participate nor interpret the story	Illustrates a picture representing the story	Illustrates a picture which truly represents the story	

Follow-up Activities

Learners can make stick puppets of the characters (see activity in this guide) and use them to dramatize and retell the story in their own words.

Learners can compare and contrast the time period and setting within the story with today's world and setting.

Self-Assessment (To be completed after the lesson.)

Think about your delivery of the lesson. What went well? What would you change? Was the amount of time allotted for the lesson sufficient? Did you need more or less time? Review the lesson objectives. Did the students meet (or exceed) the objectives or not? Why? List a few ideas on how you could make this lesson better.

LITERARY GENRE

Genre is a category, a type, a class, or a selection of literature. There are many literary genres including: Historical fiction; Science fiction; Mystery, Poetry, Biography, Autobiography; Informational, Picture book, Chapter book, Folklore, Fantasy, Humor, and Contemporary realism to name a few. Children should have exposure to various types of literary genre to help them extend their interests and knowledge.

PLOT

The PLOT of the story is the structured plan of action and the series of events within the story. The plot plan could include drama, specific events, themes, mystery, a journey, struggle or conflict, suspense and tension, moral decisions, and may deal with personal growth or societal issues. Plots are often centered around the protagonist (hero), the action, conflict and antagonism, or equally on two or more characters (dualist plot).

There are a number of **Plot patterns:**

- Linear plot pattern – events progress logically and simply
- Step by step pattern – events follow a logical progression that reach a climax and lead to a gratifying and expected ending
- Circular – events progress from the beginning and continue and end at the same location
- Modified circular - events begin and end in at nearly the same location
- Turn-about – events progress logically while leading to an unexpected conclusion
- Repetitive – events reoccur throughout the story

From Hennings, (2002) in Braunius, Palenzuela, & Leistner (2004)

THEME

The theme is the main idea for the story. The theme reveals the author's purpose for writing the story. There are numerous themes in children's literature. Some common ones include: friendship, growing up or coming of age, overcoming conflicts and obstacles, conquering fears, defeating prejudice, , nature, acceptance of self and/or others, and solving problems.

SETTING

The setting in a narrative story is the moment of time or the "when of the story" and the location or the "where of the story." The time period can be a specific hour, day, week, season, year, or interval. A setting can be in present time, in the past, or in the future. The "location" can be a certain select place, a country, or any locale.

Settings can be either backdrop settings or integral and vital to the story. A backdrop setting is often vague and less specific and does not significantly affect the plot or the characters in the story. A vital setting often is more fully described and affects the plot and influences how the characters live or what they do in the story.

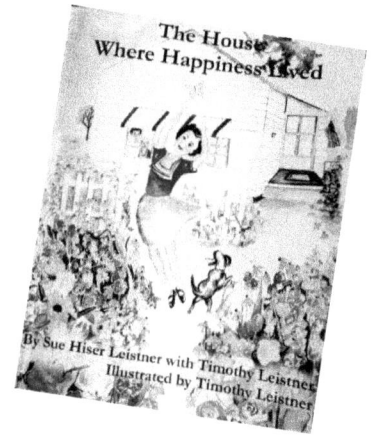

What is the setting for **"The House Where Happiness Lived"**?

_____

_____

_____

_____

_____

_____

Is this setting vital to the story or a backdrop setting and why?

_____

_____

_____

_____

_____

Describe the time period when this story takes place. How is the same and how is it

different than present day?

_____

_____

_____

_____

_____

CHARACTERIZATION

The characters are the essential figures within a story and for whom the action takes place. There is often a central figure (the protagonist) along with supporting characters in children's literature. In "The House Where Happiness Lived" the main character is the "Child of Happiness" and supporting characters are Grandma, Mama, and Scrap. Secondary characters include Wade, Wade's mother, the Tramp, and the Ice Man.

Authors use a number of formulas to reveal and develop the characters in a story to the reader:

- Through Narration – describing and telling the reader about the characters
- Through spoken conversations, discussion or dialogue among the characters
- Through describing the thoughts of the character
- Through describing the thoughts of others about the character
- Through actions and deeds

FORMAT

The format of a book includes the book's cover, shape, size, paper quality, texture, binding, spine, number of pages, and length of the book. The format actually deals with all of the physical aspects of a book. This would also include the text features and typography (type and size of font), the printed words and the illustrations, along with any unique characteristics of the book (such as die cuts, textural materials, built in sounds or lighting, or things like wheels on the book). Digital text and electronic version books (e-books) also have special alternate formats including size and shape considerations, compression options, special software and user devices, and readability.

The format of a book needs to be considered by both parents and teachers in regards to the child who will be reading the book. There are many questions to consider. Should the book have a hard cover vs. a soft cover? When are wordless books (those with illustrations only) best used? Is using a Big Book (those with an enlarged font and illustrations) best for larger audiences?

Format is especially important in regards to the age of the child. Infants and toddlers enjoy board books, cloth books, and plastic wipe off books that they can manipulate. Younger children like colorful well-illustrated and durable picture books, with characters that they may relate to. Elementary age children like to connect to characters. They like a larger font than what is typically displayed in older children and adults' books. Some special needs children may require an adaptive specialized format, such as those with audible formats, electronic books, Large Print enlarged fonts, talking books, devices to aid in turning the pages, and those with added alternative formats.

The format is also an important consideration depending on where and how the book will be used and how assessable the books are to children. Books read at home may have two to ten hands on them on any given day, while this may multiple 25 percent or more in the classroom! The format of a book is an important consideration and individual teachers and parents should decide what format is best for their children and situation.

Children's Book Review & Evaluation Form

Book Title: _____

Author(s): _____

Illustrator(s): _____

Publisher & Year of Publication: _____

Age Appropriate Level (Consider the content and readability level):

_____

Describe the Genre(s):

_____

_____

Plot & Plot Pattern:

_____

_____

Setting - Is the setting integral or backdrop and why?:

_____

_____

Characterization:

_____

_____

Theme:

_____

_____

Format:

_____

_____

Type of illustration:

_____

_____

Your Personal Opinion of the book:

_____

_____

Part II: Useful Activities to Increase Understanding

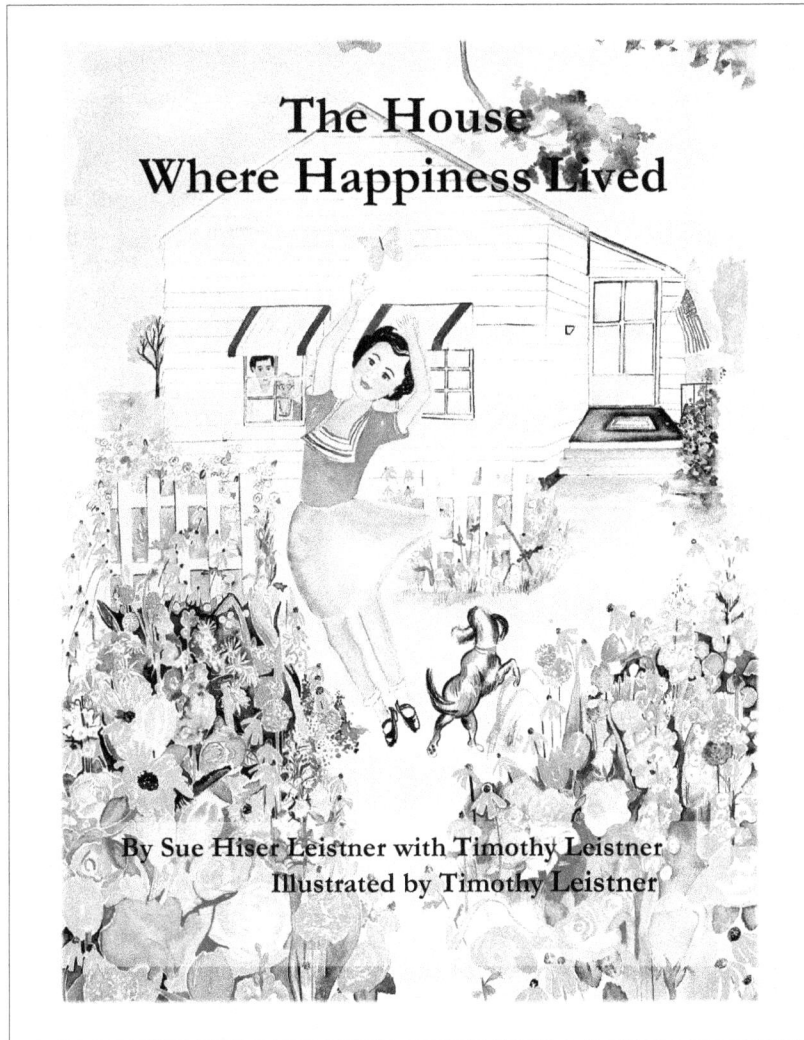

The House
Where Happiness Lived

By Sue Hiser Leistner with Timothy Leistner
Illustrated by Timothy Leistner

UNIQUE WORDS

Some words may be challenging or unfamiliar to children. The words may be "unique" to them. Share this list of vocabulary words from the book, "**The House Where Happiness Lived**" with children and discuss each of the word's meanings.

Unique Word:	Definition:	Parts of speech:
Cottage	A small simple house. A dwelling, hut, shack or cabin.	Noun (A person, place, or thing)
Gems	A precious or semiprecious stone when cut and polished.	Noun (A person, place, or thing)
Kaleidoscope	A toy with a tube containing mirrors and pieces of colored glass or paper, whose reflections will produce changing patterns.	Noun (A person, place, or thing)
Bobby Pin	A kind of sprung hairpin or small clip.	Noun (A person, place, or thing)
Tramp	A person who travels from place to place on foot in search of work or as a vagrant or beggar.	Noun (A person, place, or thing)
Poises	A small bunch of fresh flowers.	Noun (A person, place, or thing)
Hermit	Any person living in solitude or seeking to do so. A recluse.	Noun (A person, place, or thing)
President Roosevelt	The 32nd President of the United States of America. He was elected four times and instituted the New Deal to counter the Great Depression. He led the country during World War II.	Noun (A person, place, or thing)
Swell	Excellent; very well.	Adverb
Stoop	Exterior steps and landing at the entrance to a doorway.	Noun (A person, place, or thing)

UNIQUE WORDS MATCHING ACTIVITY

DRAW A LINE TO MATCH THE "UNIQUE WORD" TO THE CORRECT PICTURE

Bobby Pin

Cottage

Gems

Hermit

Ice Truck

Kaleidoscope

Poises

President Roosevelt

Tramp

Stoop

WRITING ACTIVITY
Comprehension

In our book, the "Child of Happiness" did many things that made the people in her life happy. Reread and review the happenings in the story. Write some of the things she did to make others' happy. How did doing these things make her feel? Why?

_____

_____

_____

_____

_____

_____

_____

_____

_____

_____

_____

_____

_____

Now, write your own list of things YOU can do which will make someone happy.

"My make someone HAPPY" list:

RHYMING WORDS

Children love to play word games.
Say a few words from our story along with a rhyming word.
Example:

1) **House** & Mouse
2) **Curls** & Twirls
3) **Pin** & Win

Choose more words from the story. Have children come up with words that rhyme with them. Develop phonemic knowledge by creating and playing this Rhyming Button Game. Here's how:

- Cut BUTTON shapes. Mount on heavy card stock paper.
- Write a word on the front and a word that rhymes with it on the back of each button.
- The children take turns picking a button; reading the word; and saying a word that rhymes with it. Turn the button over and see if you guessed the hidden rhyming word.
- This can be an individual or small group activity
- Concentrate on reading the words and hearing the thymes.

BUTTON TEMPLATES

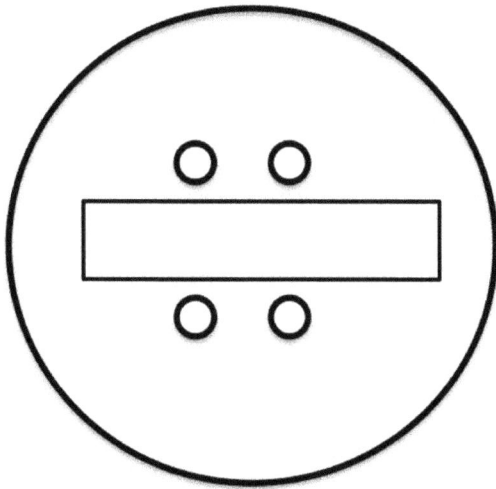

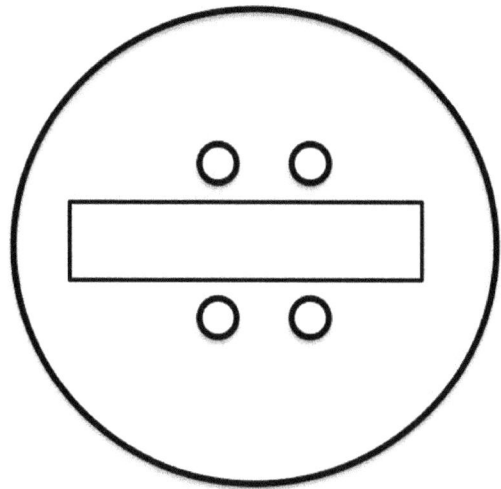

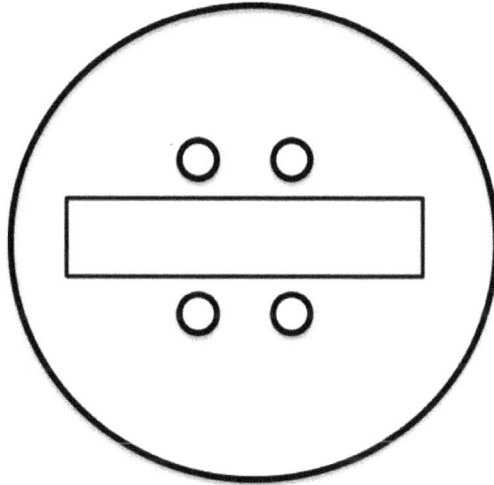

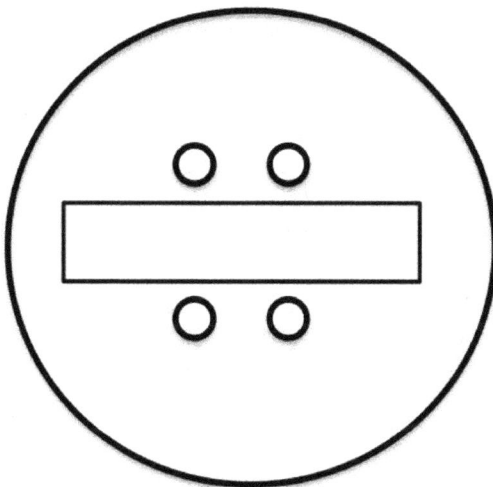

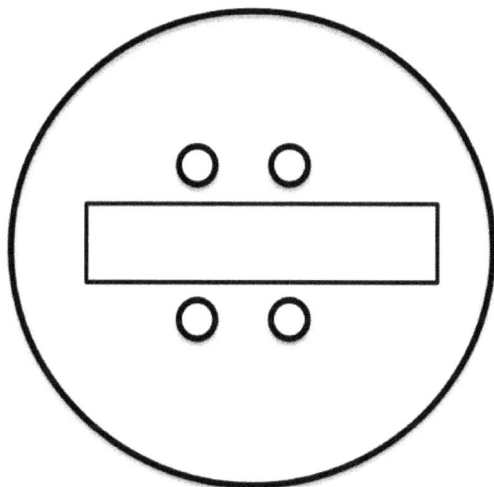

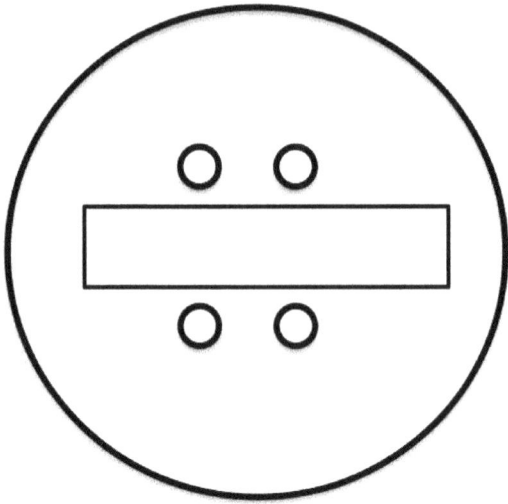

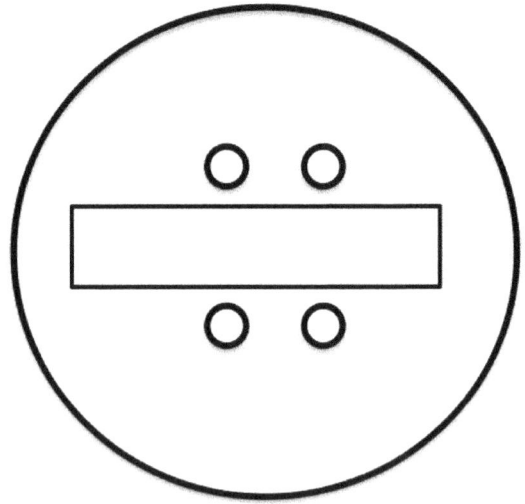

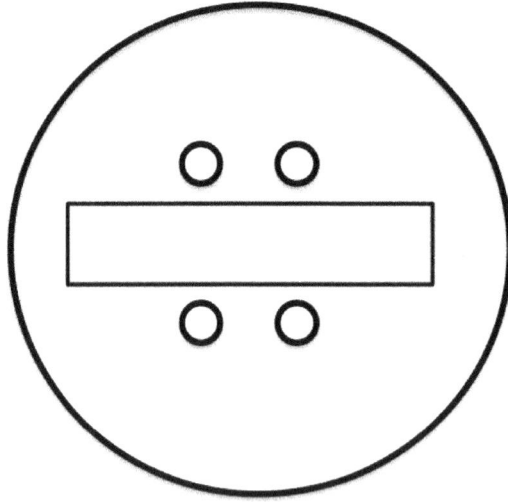

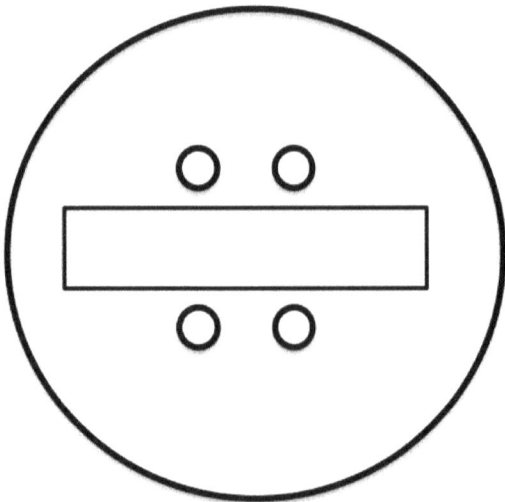

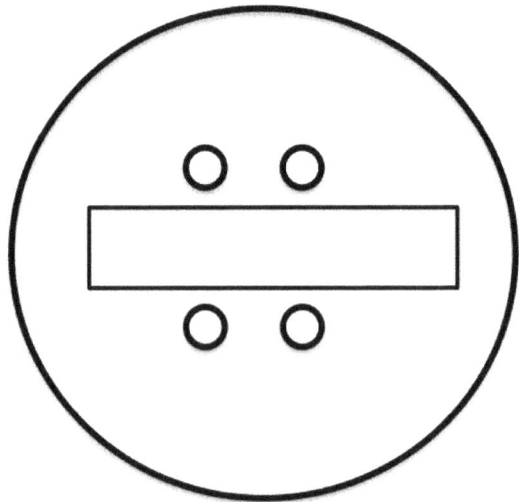

POETRY

How do you feel when you're happy?
Write an acrostic poem using the word "HAPPINESS."

H _____ _____

A _____

P _____

P _____

I _____

N _____

E _____

S _____

S _____

LET'S GET COOKING!
Thinking & Illustration Activity

The "Child of Happiness" and her grandma cooked a meal of eggs and potatoes in an iron skillet for the "tramp" that came to their door asking for food. What would you cook for a person who was hungry and in need of a meal? Draw a picture of it in the skillet below.

INVESTIGATE MORE ABOUT THE SETTING:
Social Studies Integration

The setting for **"The House Where Happiness Lived"** is in the past. This story may be considered "historical fiction" because of the time period it is set, although it was based on the lives of real life people. The time period for our story is set in the late 1930's during the Great Depression in the USA. Franklin Delano Roosevelt was the president at this time. He is referred to within the story. Discussion: How does the time period affect the characters, how they live, and what they do in the story?

Investigate: Find out more about President Franklin Delano Roosevelt (FDR) and the times of the Great Depression.

President Franklin Delano Roosevelt (FDR)

MAKE A DIORAMA
Setting Activity

In the book, **"The House Where Happiness Lived"** the setting is a small white house (or a cottage) where the "Child of Happiness," Mama, and Grandma lived. Make a diorama to depict the setting of the story.

Materials needed:
- A shoebox
- Scissors
- Glue
- Paper
- Crayons, markers, or colored pencils

Here's how:
Make a quick sketch to design your diorama here. Create your diorama with the materials listed above.

FURTHER INVESTIGATION ABOUT THE SETTING & TIMELINE ACTIVITY:
Social Studies (History) Integration

Investigate: Find out more about the times of the Great Depression. Create a timeline of The Great Depression to better understand the events of this time period and its importance in history. The Great Depression was an extremely difficult time for people living in the USA and lasted from 1929-1941.

The Great Depression Write the Event	Year 1929-1941	Find or draw a picture that represents this period.

MAKE TULIP POISES
Art Activity

The setting for "**The House Where Happiness Lived**" is a small white house (cottage) that was surrounded by flowers -"Tulips, Daisies and Black Eyed Susan's." Make your own flowers out of tissue paper, pipe cleaners, and scrap materials. Here's an art activity to create tulips from egg cartons.

Materials needed:

- **Egg carton**
- **Scissors**
- **Pipe cleaners**
- **Buttons**

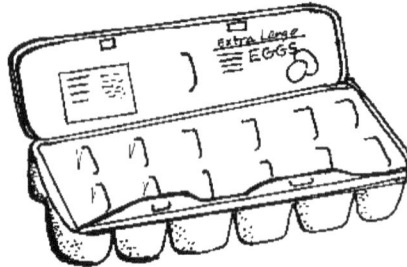

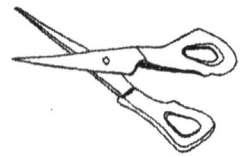

Optional:

- **Paints and brushes**

Using your scissors cut each eggcup section out of the egg carton. See how they look like tulip petals? With your scissors, carefully poke two small holes in the bottom of each "tulip" cup. Loop a pipe cleaner (with a button attached for the flower center) through the two holes. Twist the pipe cleaner to create the stem.

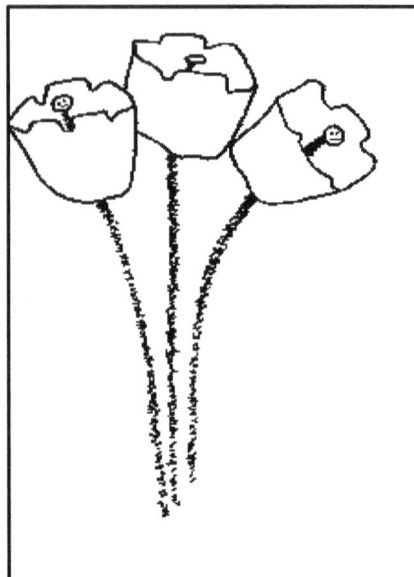

PAINT A "HAPPINESS GARDEN"
Art Activity

The house in the book, **"The House Where Happiness Lived"** was surrounded by beautiful flower gardens. Create your own painting of a flower garden.

Materials needed:

- Watercolor paper (140 lb.)
- Paint brushes
- Watercolor paints
- Craft Tissue Paper
- Scissors
- Water

Here's how:

Cut flower petal shapes (circles, ovals, leaves) from the tissue paper. Set aside.
Use water and a paintbrush to wet the entire front side of your watercolor paper.
Gently set each tissue paper flower shape on top of the wet paper surface.
The color from the tissue paper will "bleed" into the paper.
Take the remaining wet tissue off of the paper surface and discard.
Use paints and brushes to paint into the flower shapes to enhance your painting.
Share your painting with a friend or family member

PLANT A FLOWER GARDEN
Earth Science Integration Activity

"The House Where Happiness Lived" was surrounded by flower gardens.
Start your own flower garden! Plant seeds and watch them grow!

Materials needed:

- Flower seeds (assortment)
- Soil
- Flower pot (or cup)
- Water
- Sunlight

Here's how:

Fill your flowerpot (or cup) about half full with soil. Using your finger, push a small indentation (hole) in the soil. Place the flower seeds in the hole. Cover with soil. Add water. Place in the sunlight. Watch over days to see the flower seeds sprout and grow!

DANCING BUTTERFLY
Art Activity

In our story, "**The House Where Happiness Lived,**" the Child of Happiness "chased a dancing butterfly." Design and create your own dancing butterfly art.

Materials needed:

- Standard Round Coffee Filter
- Markers (or water color paints)
- Clothespin
- Pipe cleaner
- String

Procedure:

Gather the coffee filter from the middle to form the butterfly wings.

Clip the clothespin on for the butterfly's body.

Attach the pipe cleaner for the butterfly's antenna.

Use marker (or watercolor paints) to design the colors of the wings.

Tie on the string. Dance with your butterfly!

COLLECTIONS

Writing and Visually Representing Activity

In the book, "**The House Where Happiness Lived**" the "Child of Happiness" collected colorful pieces of broken glass that she called, "gems". She loved making button necklaces using the buttons from her Grandma's collection of buttons in the button bucket. Her friend, Wade collected comic books.

Many people collect things. Some people collect coins or stamps. Some collect art or dolls or something else. What do you collect? Tell about it.

My Name is: _____

What do you collect?

_____

When did you start collecting?

_____

How do you find the things for your collection?

_____

Why do you collect what you do?

_____

Draw a picture of your collection:

The "Child of Happiness" shared her collection of "gems" with her friend, Wade. He shared his collection of comic books with her. Share your collection with a friend, at school, or with a special person in your family.

COLLECTIONS

BUTTONS,
BUTTONS,
AND
MORE
BUTTONS!

Make your own Button Necklace to share with someone special.

Materials needed:
- **Buttons (an assortment)**
- **Large craft needle**
- **String or thread**

Procedure:
Using your craft needle, string each button onto the thread. Tie a large knot at the end. Give your necklace to someone special and share happiness!

MAKE YOUR OWN COMIC BOOK SUPER HERO

In our story, Wade collected and shared his comic books. Comic books are also called "funny pages." They are usually humorous short stories or about super heroes and characters with super human powers. Develop your own character or super hero:

List Character Traits:
_____

List any super human powers or feats they accomplish:
_____

What does your character look like? Draw a picture of your character or superhero in the frame below:

MY SUPER HERO

CREATE YOUR OWN COMIC STRIP

Put your character into your own comic strip: Draw illustrations and words. Now put it all together in your own comic strip! Use CALL OUT shapes for dialogue and CLOUDS above for thoughts.

"GEMS"
Collage Art Activity

The "Child of Happiness" found bits of broken glass that she called, "gems" and collected them in an old cigar box. Make "GEMS" Collage Art.

Materials needed:
- **Colorful tissue papers and/or cellophane papers (an assortment of colors)**
- **Heavy craft paper or poster board**
- **Scissors**
- **Modge Podge or glue sealant**
- **Paint Brush**

Procedure:
Cut the tissue paper and cellophane paper into a variety of free form shapes. Using Modge Podge and a brush, glue each of the shapes onto the craft paper to create a collage.

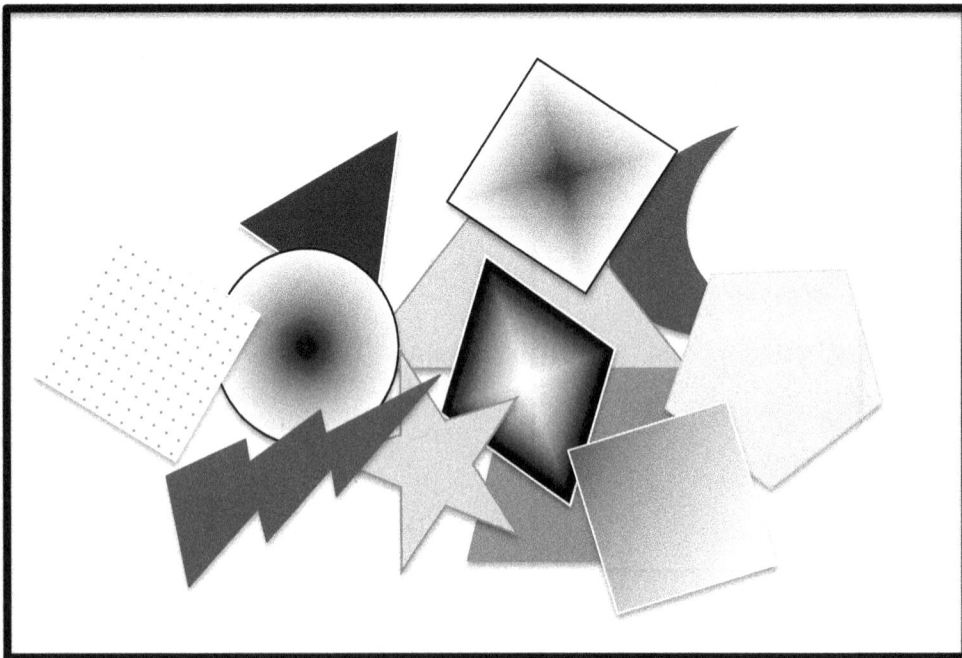

♪ MUSIC ♪

Sing a new song of "Happiness." Think of a familiar classic song you like to sing… such as the old French tune, "Twinkle, Twinkle, Little Star." Count the syllables in each line to help keep the rhythm and beat. Now think of things that make people happy and using that tune, come up with new lyrics for a new song.

Example:

Lyrics	Number of syllables per line
Twinkle, Twinkle Little Star	7
How I wonder what you are!	7
Up above the world so high	7
Like a diamond in the sky	7
Twinkle, Twinkle, Little Star	7
How I wonder what you are!	7

Here is a model of a new song:

Happy, Happy, Joyful Me	7
Kindness makes me shout with glee!	7
Being caring to my friends	7
Creates smiles which never end	7
Happy, Happy, Joyful Me	7
Kindness makes me shout with glee!	7

-TL (2013)

Now, create your own song!

Note: The tune and lyrics to "Twinkle, Twinkle, Little Star" supposedly is from the 1765 traditional song from Paris, France and is listed as public domain.

RECIPE FOR MAKING ICE CHIPS

The "Child of Happiness" sipped on an **ICE CHIP** while she waited for her mother at the bus stop. She got the ice chip from the Ice Man. You can make your own kind of **ICE CHIP**.

Needed materials:
- Water
- Ice cube tray
- Popsicle sticks
- Freezer

Here's how:
- Fill the ice cube tray with water.
- Place a Popsicle stick in each opening.
- Place the ice cube tray in your freezer. Freeze over night.
- Pop the ice chips from the tray. Sip and enjoy!
- Optional: Add your favorite fruit flavoring to the water.

CREATE YOUR OWN FAMILY FRAME
Art Activity

The "Child of Happiness" lived with her Mama, Grandma, and her dog, Scrap. She kept pictures of her family on a night table by her bed. Who is your family? Make a special FAMILY FRAME for a photograph of your family.

Needed materials:

- **4 Large Popsicle sticks (tongue depressors)**
- **Glue**
- **Uncooked Macaroni noodles**
- **Gold spray paint**
- **Family Photograph**

Here's how:

- **Glue the Popsicle sticks together to form a square frame.**
- **Glue the macaroni noodles onto the stick frame creating a design. Allow to dry.**
- **Spray paint the frame. (adult supervision is needed)**
- **Place your family photograph inside your frame.**

Optional: Glue Buttons or gems onto your picture frame.

A MONTH OF FUN FAMILY ACTIVITIES TO DO

"THE HOUSE WHERE HAPPINESS LIVED"
Language Arts Activities

SUNDAY	MONDAY	TUESDAY	WEDNESDAY	THURSDAY	FRIDAY	SATURDAY
The "Child of Happiness" shared happiness. Make a list of things you can do to make others' happy.	Read a poem today that makes you feel happy.	Think about alternate words (synonyms) for the word "Happiness". Use your dictionary to find at least five words that mean "Happiness." Write them in your journal.	Write a "Thank You" note to a special person who has helped you. Tell them why you appreciate what they did!	Share a family picture album and talk about your Family Memories. What makes you and your family happy?	The "Child of Happiness" lived with Mama, Grandma, and her dog, Scrap. Who do you live with? Draw an illustration of YOUR FAMILY.	Parents: Show your child a picture of yourself when you were his/her age. Compare your picture with their picture and discuss the similarities and differences.
The setting for "The House Where Happiness Lived" was in a little white house of the corner. Where do you live? Draw an illustration of your home.	In "The House Where Happiness Lived," the style of the buildings, vehicles, and dress are different than today's styles. Compare the illustrations in the book to today's style. Talk about the differences and similarities.	People live in different types of homes. Research and read about the different types of family dwellings (Apartments, condominiums, teepees, igloos, huts, houseboats and such). Compare how they are similar and how they are different.	In our story, "The House Where Happiness Lived" the house was surrounded by beautiful flower gardens. What is your favorite flower? Draw a picture of it and write 5 things you like about flowers.	The "Child of Happiness" sang POP GOES THE WEASEL and some school songs with her grandma. Sing a special school song together with a member of your family	The "Child of Happiness" liked to pick poises from her garden. Plant some flower seeds in a flowerpot or your garden. Water them, wait, and observe garden growth!	In our story, Grandma fried chicken in an iron skillet. The "Child of Happiness" helped by setting the table. Parents: Make a favorite family recipe together. Your child can help out by setting the table.

In our story, Mama read the newspaper when she got home from work. Look through your hometown newspaper. Pick out some ads from local businesses and stores. Are these businesses in your neighborhood?	The "Child of Happiness" liked to listen to scary stories with her family on the radio. Try reading a "scary " story *in the spotlight* – read with a flashlight in the dark!	Begin your own Family Newspaper. Write stories about family news and publish it for your relatives.	Find words you know in the newspaper. Cut out theses words and some pictures. Use them to make up your own "Collage Story". Materials needed: - Your newspaper, scissors, glue, & paper.	Challenge: Use your newspaper to find and circle some new words that are unfamiliar to you. Ask your teacher or family member to help you to learn these new words.	In our story, the "Child of Happiness" saw people working as she walked to the bus stop in her neighborhood. Take a neighborhood walk and see the people in your neighborhood. SMILE and be happy!	The "Child of Happiness" and her family listened to "The Hermit's Cave" radio show together. Parents: Rather than watching television tonight, listen to the radio with your family. You can even listen to "The Hermit's Cave" online!
The "Child of Happiness" collected bits of glass that she called "GEMS". She kept them in an old cigar box. Start your own collection of something you like. What type of container will you use to keep your collection together?	In our story, The Child of Happiness's friend, Wade, collected COMIC books. Read a COMIC book! Talk about the illustrations.	In our story, the "Child of Happiness" chased a butterfly. Research what plants butterflies like. Plant some of these plants in your garden.	Comic books have a lot of action in the stories and illustrations. Write your own comic strip. Use action words and illustrations with plenty of action!	Count the syllables in your whole name. Use this number to do that many kind things for someone in your life today.	Visit your local or school library. Ask your Librarian/ Media Specialist to help you locate books on collecting.	In our story, the "Child of Happiness" and her friend, Wade shared their collections. Share something you have collected with a friend or family member.
Challenge: Take an "Alphabet picture walk" through the book, "The House Where Happiness Lived." Find something from the book which starts with an A such as (Apron); B (Buttons); C (Cigar Box) and so on through Z.	During the time period of our story, Franklin Delano Roosevelt (FDR) was the 32nd President of the United States of America (1933-1945). Research this president and discuss the time period when he lived.	"The House Where Happiness Lived" is a story about a family living in their special house. What kind of house do you want to live in? Draw a picture of your house in the future.				

FURTHER READING:

"The House Where Happiness Lived" is a family story about a child, her mama, grandma, and dog who lived in their house during the times of the Great Depression. Read additional children's picture books (both old and new) with the word "House" in the title. Here are few great suggestions:

TITLE:	AUTHOR:	ILLUSTRATOR:	PUBLISHED:
The Little House	Virginia Lee Burton	Virginia Lee Burton	1942 Caldecott Medal
The House in the Night	Susan Marie Swanson	Beth Krommes	2008 Caldecott Medal
A House for Hermit Crab	Eric Carle	Eric Carle	1991
Butterfly House	Eve Bunting	Greg Shed	1999
In My Mother's House	Ann Nolan Clark	Velino Herrera	1992
Little House in the Big Woods	Laura Ingalls Wilder	Garth Williams	1932
This Is The House That Jack Built (First version)	Randolph Caldecott	Randolph Caldecott	1887
This Is The House That Jack Built	Simms Taback	Simms Taback	2004
The House At Pooh Corner	A.A. Milne	Ernest H. Shepard	1928/ 1992
In A People House	Dr. Seuss	Dr. Seuss	2007

HOUSE MAKING ACTIVITY AND TEMPLATE

Cut along the outer lines and fold the dotted lines.   Construct and color the House.

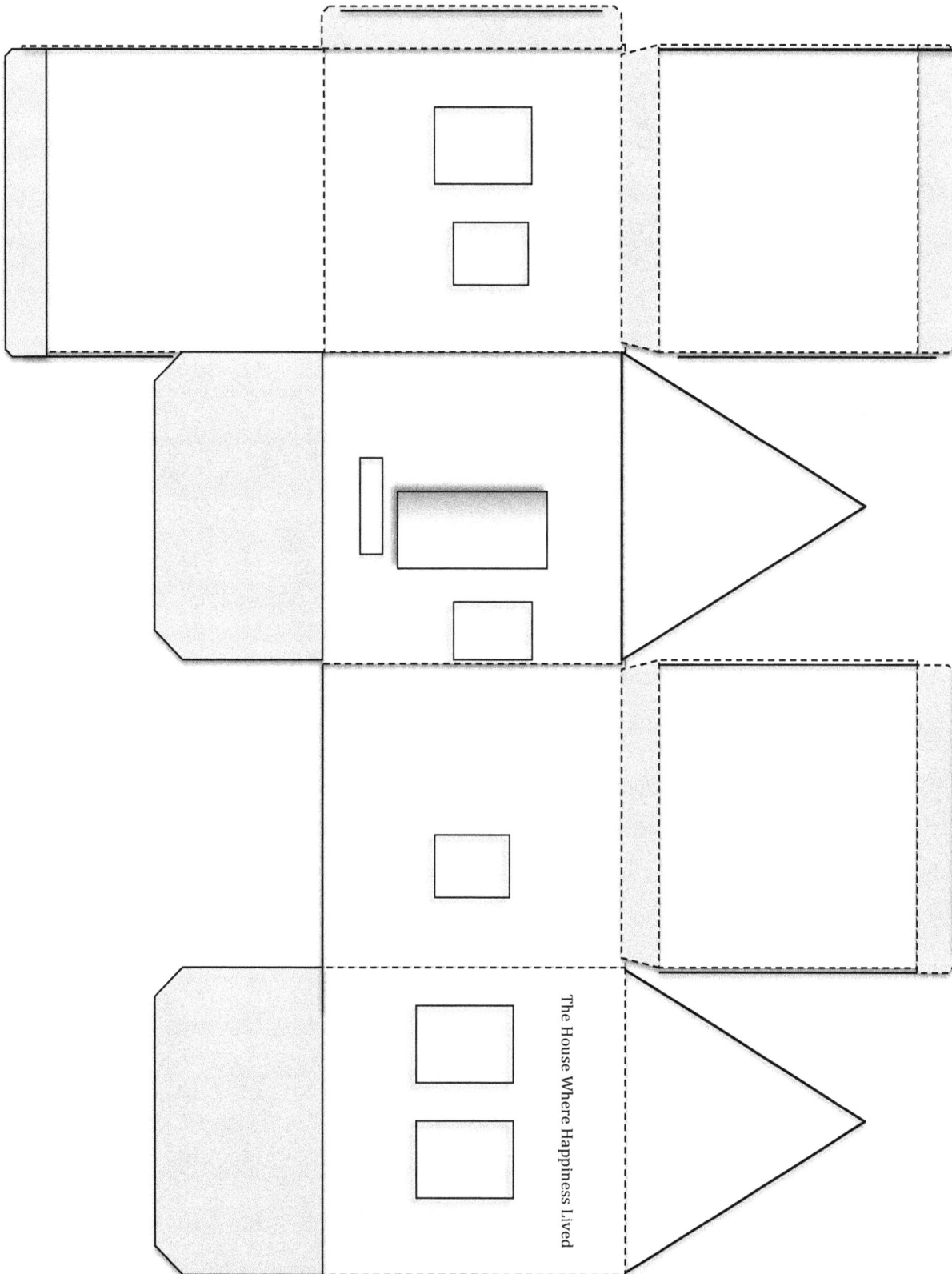

The House Where Happiness Lived

MAKE A "HAPPINESS HOUSE" BOOKMARK

Create your own bookmark. Write a message on it
and draw a picture of something that
or someone who makes you happy!

Needed materials:

- Bookmark template
- Heavy paper (card stock)
- Scissors
- Crayons, markers, or colored pencils

Here's how:

- Cut out the bookmark shape using this template.
- Write a message on it that makes you happy.
- Decorate with crayons, markers, or colored pencils.
- Enjoy using your bookmark.

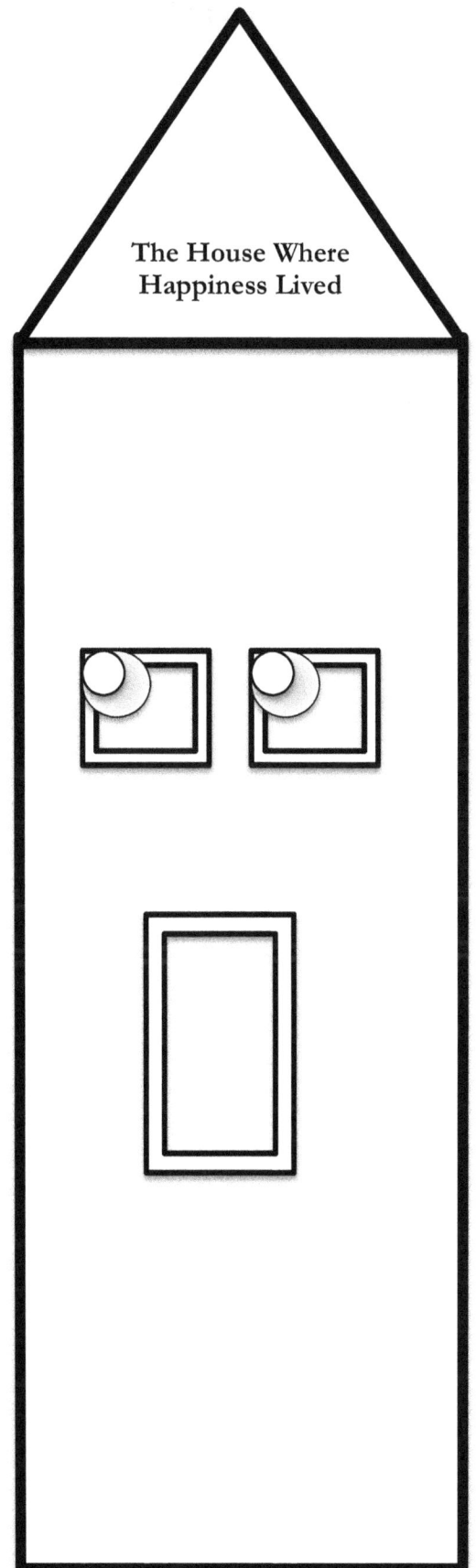

The House Where
Happiness Lived

MAKE A "SHARE HAPPINESS" AWARD RIBBON

"The Child of Happiness"
shared happiness with others.
Color and cut out this Award
Ribbon. Present it to someone
special who has done kind
deeds and shares happiness!

SHARE
HAPPINESS

STORY CHARACTERS

Make your own Character stick puppets from the book, "The House Where Happiness Lived." Color and cut out each character. Use a craft stick and glue to attach the characters to the sticks. Make other characters from the story. Use your puppets to retell (dramatize) the story in your own words.

"Grandma"

"Mama" with the "Child of Happiness"

"Scrap"

ABOUT THE AUTHORS

Sue Hiser Leistner and Timothy Leistner, the authors and illustrator of "The House Where Happiness Lived" are a mother and son team. They worked together writing the story prior to the illustrations being completed.

Sue Hiser Leistner worked as a freelance writer, contributing articles to The Toledo Blade Newspaper, Indianapolis Star, Mature Living Magazine, and others. She has interviewed such notable celebrities such as the American advice columnist, Ann Landers, Reverend Billy Graham, Tennis professional, Bobby Riggs and others. She wrote her own informational and humorous column, "Sincerely Sue," for Ohio-Michigan Line Magazine for many years.

Timothy Leistner, Ed.D., originally from Ohio, now resides in Florida and teaches courses on Children's Literature and Language Arts at Florida Atlantic University. He co-authored the textbook, "Exploring Language Arts through Literature: Birth –Grade 8." He is an accomplished award winning visual artist who has developed art programs for special needs populations, adults, and children. He is a member of Society for Children's Book Writers and Illustrators.

References:

Braunius, M., Palenzuela, S., & Leistner, T. (2004). Exploring language arts through literature: Birth-grade 8. Dubuque, IA: Kendall/Hunt Publishing Company.

Hennings, D. (2002). Communication in action: Teaching literature-based language arts (8th ed.). Boston: Houghton Mifflin Company.

Leistner, S. H., & Leistner, T. (2013). The house where happiness lived. Button Bucket Books.

The New York State Education Department. (2013). *Learning Standards for English as a second language. Learning standards and performance indicators.* New York, NY: Retrieved from www.nysed.gov

National Council of Teachers of English. (2013). *NCTE/IRA Standards for English Language Arts.* Urbana, IL: Retrieved October 17, 2013, from www.ncte.org

National Governors Association Center for Best Practices, Council of Chief State School officers, (2010). *Common core state standards.* Washington, D.C.: Retrieved October 19, 2013 from www.corestandards.org

State of Florida, Department of State. (1996). *Florida Curriculum Framework Language Arts PreK-12; Goal 3 Standards.* Tallahassee, FL: Retrieved October 17, 2013, from www.paec.org/resources/FloridaCurriculumFrameworks/main/frameworks/language_arts/la all.pdf

Twinkle, Twinkle, Little Star. (-1765). Traditional folk song. Paris, France: Public domain.

Button Bucket Books

www.ingramcontent.com/pod-product-compliance
Lightning Source LLC
Chambersburg PA
CBHW062055090426
42740CB00016B/3144